I0150069

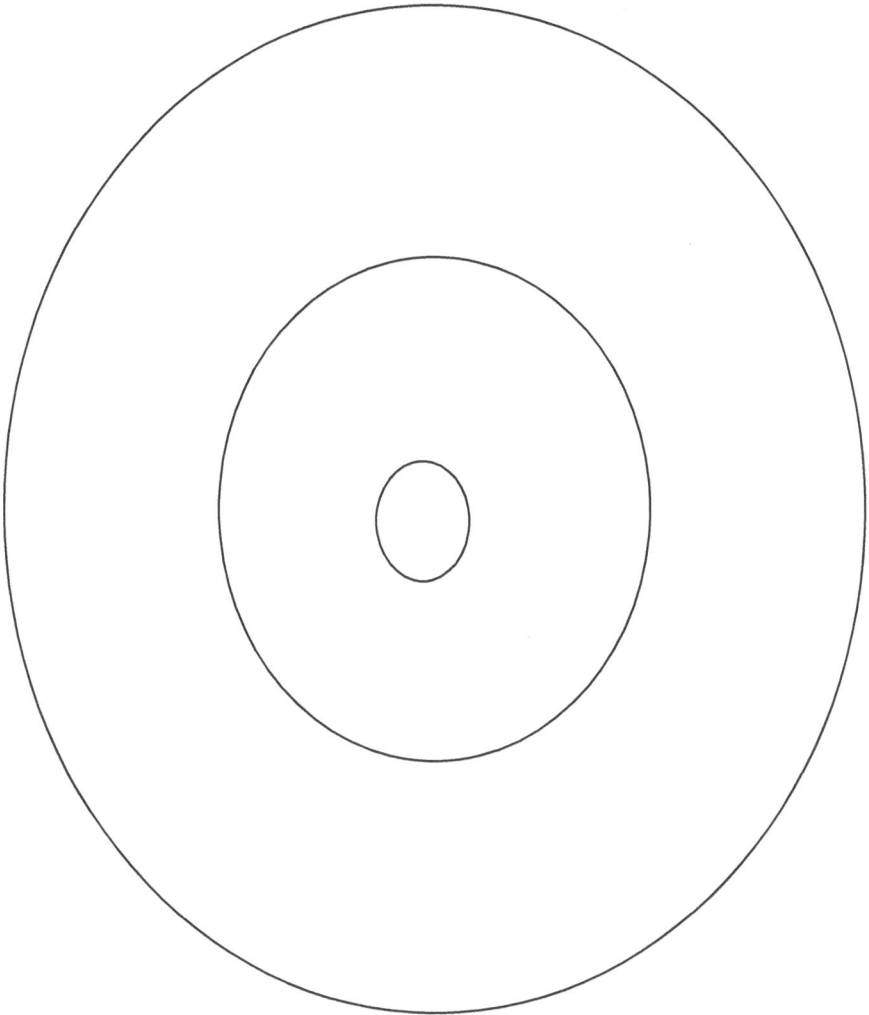

Scientific Evidence
GOD EXISTS

Written By
Mylia Tiye Mal Jaza

Scientific Evidence
GOD EXISTS

Written By
Mylia Tiye Mal Jaza

Edited By
Mari Michelle Jefferson

Art By
Ronny "Rone" Myles

Scientific Evidence God Exists

Publisher
BePublished.Org
An Initiative of The Writers Consortium
A Division of The Conglomerate

Mississippi Mail Center
P.O. Box 8324
Jackson, MS 39284-8324

Dallas Publishing Office
PH (972) 880-8316
FX (267) 821-8316
mari@bepublished.org

Softcover ISBN: 978-0-6151-6333-8

Printed in the United States of America

First Edition

Dedication

With love beyond mine
To family, truth seekers, all others ever endowed
With life, even temporarily and yet to come,
In praise to Jah
(God, Yahweh, Jehovah, Yeshua, Jesus, Holy Spirit)

Table of Contents

Introduction

With all my heart, I thank you for picking up this book, and thank Jah for blessing me to write it. SCIENTIFIC EVIDENCE GOD EXISTS is borne from the hope that every aspect of life revealed works to incite enlightenment in the lives of others.

These personal reflections and realizations that God exists have afforded me the ability to achieve so much and endure even more despite my youthfulness and age. Because of this, I feel bad for anyone so misled or confused that they are unable to experience the peace found in embracing God and believing things will indeed be better at that later time because of God's sole control.

SCIENTIFIC EVIDENCE GOD EXISTS is not a work filled with footnotes, or any plethora of references to secondary works. It is simply a representation of my own journey to an acceptable answer to inquiry into the existence of a Supreme Being, The One, The Creator.

Proof is often found through researching circumstances under which relative information was released. Traversing this path has not been easy, neither has maintaining my selected course been without pain or disappointments. Nonetheless, I am certain of my conclusion, and I believe the testimonies contained here will serve to assist others in their search for an answer and even more with their search for truth.

I overstand that truth is a matter of perception, promise, passion and personality. I too understand that truth remains truth despite being denied or despised. Two people standing beside each other and the entire while are looking at the same portion of sky might disagree on whether the weather seems to suggest a clear day or coming rain, and if the color of the sky was more blue and white or grey and black. Flipping that same type token, two believers looking at the same verses from the Holy Word and at the same time the minister is reading it aloud are likely to disagree about the meanings/interpretations of the words present and the messages the preacher offers.

Therefore, it is to be expected that this work will both be accepted and rejected as one more offering of a heavily-debated belief. Still, it is because of our mortal preferences for denial and Jah's perpetual forgiveness of our battery of ordered, divine, feminine and masculine aspects of life that I was most motivated to devise this tome in response to frequently entertaining the question, "How do you know God exists?" SCIENTIFIC EVIDENCE GOD EXISTS is my way of proving He, She, It, Him, Her and Them.

On Science

To many scientists, what matters and can be presented as fact or theory is what has been noted, experienced and proven to work pretty much no matter what. This type of approach has proven useful to them to substantiate many claims and introduce new schools of thought. As a result, I felt taking a scientific approach to proving the existence of God would be most in order since my goal is to enact a way that crosses genre, industry, government and church lines to share my belief in God with those seeking comprehension, clarification and confirmation.

From a science perspective, research to establish a theory begins when observations have been made, insight has been gained, and a hypothesis has been developed for use as a basis for experimentation. After experiments are completed, the data is then gathered and assessed. Further testing then commences and the theory is finally formalized.

To many, the hypothesis has to be formulated in a matter that enables rational testing that can logically establish accuracy – i.e., if the theory can predict things that can be proven as correct or false. As a result, the overall scientific method involves a wide array of approaches.

In SCIENTIFIC EVIDENCE GOD EXISTS, the scientific method will be used as a public bay of perspective instead of a single testing method or a deliberate attempt to be in keeping with any individual or specific scientific method. The steps used here were obtained through cursory research. I selected a few common steps of scientific methods and will use them as a way to divide this book of testimonials into an easy-to-reference format.

On Book

Chapter One - Observation is all about some of the things seen and shares personal fly-on-the-wall expressions like the fact that I have observed far more of life's truths during my span than I ever thought I would have by 34. I have seen people pray and have prayers answered. I have also witnessed the request of prayers unfilled. I have watched people's lives be spared by what many people call coincidence but I call a blessing. I too witnessed professed atheists make profound statements of hope that seem to infer a belief in a spiritual being ultimately responsible for this all.

In Chapter Two - Hypothesis, I elaborate on my belief that God does exist, and is the source of all life including Own. In believing this, I predict that Jah will continue to demonstrate divine authority over human lives utilizing daily contact and elusiveness.

But the real meaty testimonials begin with Chapter Three - Experimentation, that is all about the different ways I observed things in the name of accepting that I just cannot say Jah exists without working to prove my claim – and doing that by asking for and expecting specific, divine knowledge and experiences to test my hypothesis that God would answer all prayers no matter the details or actual answer.

Chapter Four - Evaluation displays what my experiments revealed, and it acts as a report of my evaluation of the new data collected and perspective gained during the experiment/searching phases.

Chapter Five - Testing speaks about how, before forming my hypothesis into a theory, I conducted a tertiary experimental phase of openness with the mindset to determine whether the information gained is mostly contrary to data previously collected or divulges similar data as the first series of tests. In summary, it is my confirmation section further explaining how I formed the theory I hope can be used to bring more people to a relationship with Jah/God.

This notion is detailed in Chapter Six - Theory, wherein I am explaining how considering and accepting the lessons throughout my life, I conclude that the Holy Spirit helped me see that God is the real source of all life and has manifested as our Messiah. I theorize that anyone doubting God exists can sincerely pray to know the truth about this question and anything else desired or required. Fact is, my life and yours serve as prominent proof to combat any possible argument against notions that there is SCIENTIFIC EVIDENCE GOD EXISTS.

Chapter One

Observation

I have observed many of life's truths during my span. I have seen people pray and have prayers answered. I have also witnessed the request of prayers unfilled. I have watched people's lives be spared by what many people call coincidence but I call a blessing.

Additionally, I have seen people who never recognize any type of deity experience life's ups and downs with a sense of certainty regarding a positive outcome (faith). I have also witnessed professed atheists make profound statements of hope that seem to infer a belief in a spiritual being ultimately responsible for this all.

Observation of characteristics, details and events is the first step of the scientific method. It is understood that if attentiveness leads to curiosity or expressed questions, that's perfect because the questions will lead to the answers. To lack bias or rushed judgment and be as objective as possible while playing my own on-looker, I chose to seek multiple sources that are not already related or affiliated to get the most honest responses and increase the likelihood of accurate answers. I really wanted to minimize my chances of believing any more lies than I fell for in the past.

The questions of whether God exists and what human existence really means are questions I pondered early in life, every person wonders about at least once in his or her own life, and some cogitate until death. Reared in a Holiness church in the country before relocating to the city and joining a Baptist church, by adulthood I'd seen people of all religious backgrounds saying they were better than everyone else, yet they acted just like everybody else – making it impossible for me to see where the big difference and superiority laid.

My eyes drank them all until I was drunk off religion, mythology, history, life, hardship and doubt. Once truth materialized and overstanding was gained, I began fellowshipping with other Christians, Hebrew Israelites and believers in general by also attending services with my friends and relatives who were members of non-denominational, Catholic, AME, Muslim, Pentecostal, and other religious congregations. Although it was during adolescence that I began to study not only the Holy Bible but also other works of historical, scientific and mystical perspectives including the Qur'an (Koran), it was in adulthood that I finally had the chance to see the applications and ramifications of God-centered and man-centered beliefs.

And while I remain far from knowing everything about anything, I am confident regarding the bit of knowledge I do possess about all things. As it applies to life in general, I know that living blissfully in this world and finding/promoting truth are both near-Hell experiences (if not, are totally Hell). I also know that no matter what does or does not go my way, the few immutable facts I embrace are that God exists and, per Jah, Christ is my Messiah, the Holy Spirit is my comforting instructor, and I am made in God's image.

Atheists and Agnostics tend to get neurotic and call me brainwashed, all the while they continue to choose to promulgate the belief that all this life we see before us suddenly sprang out of nothingness at will due largely to chance and evolution. My question to them is this: "How can something evolve unless first it has existed in a noted core form that is both similar to and different from the present manifestation?" In other words, "Nothing comes from nothing, so how can there be evolution if there is not first life? Also, why aren't apes/mud/insects/fish still turning into people if that's how people materialized?"

And then there's the other group. Others who believe there is a Great One that is All's Creator, but that this entity does not get involved in the daily activities of people. Such a god, they say, would never materialize as a human to become a Messiah for the believers. That god sounds like one that doesn't love its people. That's nothing like Yahweh.

To them, I present this: Say you had a child who said you expected too much from them because you didn't understand their plight since you do not know what it's like to be in college nowadays. So, to show you are able, willing and wanting to help your child through anything (even accepting that you have unconditional love for him or her), you enrolled in college, endured the nutty and cruel professors and students, then graduated. Your child even had classes with you although your child was enrolled first, and your child witnessed your graduation ceremony and heard your valedictorian speech.

However, still a student, your child goes around denying to others that have heard about you that you proved your love through sacrifice by saying you never manifested yourself as a current-day student, let alone graduated and was the valedictorian. How would you feel? What would you do? If you're anything like

God, you'd keep giving your child chances to realize his/her and your actions and their weight, and you'll remain willing to keep forgiving that child for denying your love and causing you pain (doing this for as long as you can take the hurt generated as a result).

I long accepted that the truth of whether or not there exists an entity or being that created all life on Earth has been debated for millennia and will probably not be fully settled in my lifetime. Even today, a number of today's youth, adults and seniors doubt divine presence or even flat out believe that there is no Jah, no Yahweh, no Jehovah or Allah, no God, and definitely no Creator of any spiritual or natural worlds. After all, they conclude and ask, "If all life comes from life and we all came from God, what is the source of God's supposed life?"

I believe She is the beginning of Him, God is Them, and is thus the self-sustaining force that serves as the source of all life including planets, matter, elements, plants, animals and humans.

God is generally a mystery, and I know I won't know the full truth until my soul exists this shell and world, this I accept. Because of this, I can also understand how people have a hard time placing faith in a mystery. However, if a mystery is something that cannot be understood or explained in its entirety, how can anyone who understands the mystery enough to place faith in it as it is, not also be able to be faithful enough to maintain and share belief when it is difficult to explain it to those who have not conceded the mysterious?

Speaking from the angle of one acting as an amateur philosopher, theologian and scientist, I readily accept that some believers in the Most

High have sorted past the mysticism of tradition to find reasons and ways to believe. Some research books in an effort to find areas of inconsistency and fallacy. Others do so to allow Jah to minister directly into their lives.

I also sought out knowledge, wisdom, truth, and comprehension (and still do) to identify information I can stand under, over and beside to eliminate the things that baffled me about God. This is what I would like to encourage everyone to do - earnestly seek to find, know, accept and apply God.

I have briefly presented these actual, real-life examples and concepts to say, number one, believers and non-believers perform actions that hurt God and go against dictates for our lives – so no one person is better than the next no matter what the trophy from the competition says. Life proves that, all in all, we each do right and wrong (though sometimes more of one than the other) and we all seem to be baffled in some way at some point in time concerning many things, including Jehovah.

We also all seem to deal with a type of uncertainty and confusion over religious details and unmet expectations through various coping mechanisms. Some people, like me, choose to read every available piece of literature found and pay attention to life experiences before totally dismissing the notion that God exists.

Others have never attended any kind of religious service by choice or ever read the entire Holy Bible (let alone any other historical, scientific or religious work) before totally debunking belief in The Most High.

And then there are those who, as a youth, accepted Jesus Christ, but allowed a few bad people and experiences to posture as adequate proof that the Messiah is nothing more than the protagonist of a millennia-told story and all life just happened and was not created by a Supreme Being dwelling in a spiritual realm.

Some of everybody has seen so much in their lives to where very little is a surprise. I know that I am one who doesn't put anything past anybody because of the fact that I've seen all kinds of things from all kinds of people. And with crimes, perversions and a world of other ails seemingly reshaping societies for the worse, I see fewer and fewer people being courageous enough to put their voice and name behind the truth and the positive / correct actions that minimize societal and human destruction.

Chapter Two

Hypothesis

My belief is that God does exist, and is the source of all life including Own. I hypothesize that Our Maker will prove this existence to anyone who wants to know and seeks to find this truth. In believing this, I predict that Jah will continue to answer prayers of even those with minimal faith and demonstrate divine authority over human lives utilizing methods including daily spiritual contact, periodic elusiveness, and messages and confirmations through humans and experiences.

When attempting to answer a question, a scientist deems it critical to form a hypothesis (or, as some would say, an educated guess) regarding the question's answer. Usually, there are many possible hypotheses, but one hypothesis will likely be selected to present a single case. For many scientists, research often involves the hypothetico-inductive method where they start with a hypothesis based on observation, insight, or theory.

Officially, a hypothesis is a malleable statement of belief that has yet to be tested and is centered on the researcher's expert judgment. This hypothesis must also be subject to falsification – meaning the research needs to be set up in such a way that the scientist is able to use logical sequences to rationally conclude either that the hypothesis is correct or incorrect. In many cases, a research project may allow the scientist to accept or reject a hypothesis, and will lead to more research questions.

My hypothesis meets all this criteria, and my experience passing out 500 flyers monthly, plus ministering to others in general, leads me to believe that anyone who has spent any time sharing their belief in God with any doubter can see that they followed steps similar to those of the scientists during their ministry.

To restate it: my hypothesis is that God will hear anyone's prayer to know the truth regarding spirituality and religion – as well as anything else – and provide him or her the information and experiences needed to know for sure that God is real if only that person would sincerely and earnestly ask to know these truths. I believe God will answer all prayers no matter the details or actual answer (remember that even no action is a form of action).

I believe it is only by direct knowledge from God that I have been able to achieve a number of things that I accomplished at various stages in my life. This is the basis for my telling people that there is nothing God will not do for those who love Him – even allow them to learn AutoCAD and other computer software and programs, receive money to publish a book, and be recruited by colleges including MIT at the age of 15 because of Practice SAT scores. God continues to do drastic things for each of us every day, and that really should be proof enough for all of us that He lives.

I recall that, while at a North Dallas gym with a friend one afternoon, I finished working out on a cycling machine and went over to a stair climber unit for a 15-minute session. About five minutes into my stair climbing, this man got on the treadmill right next to me. Immediately, he began talking about: he's so depressed because of various sicknesses; he's trying to lose 150 pounds; life is hard for a white man in an America of set-asides; and the gym should give more free personal training. The one uplifting thing he could conjure to say was his confession that he is most proud of his ability to "never fall for the God or Jesus mumbo jumbo."

You already know how I responded. I told him there's no way he can really call himself an educated person or one who is seasoned with the vast experiences of life and still truly believe denying God is accurate or acceptable.

As my soap box and 15 minutes on the stair climber was winding down, he told me he never has really believed in God and that even as a child he thought that if there was a such thing as God and that Great Maker loved all people that there would be no suffering. I said something to the affect that it doesn't matter how long anyone doubts God or how long anyone has adamantly committed to be an atheist, everyone at any time can accept and apply belief in God then use that little bit of faith to begin gaining whatever proof they need to strengthen their knowledge of the fact that God does exist. I added that, despite what he may experience or see other people going through, just as he can look at the situation and say God was not there, he can also look at the same situation and say God was there.

I told him that my belief is that the greatest gift given to man is the gift of choice, and our major charges are to choose wisely, live righteously, and earnestly seek to know God with all your heart. Because of this, most times humans choose to do bad things and the atrocities we know to have taken place all display the consequences of human disobedience, sin and haughtiness.

He looked beyond intrigued. I used the moment as a chance to tell him about the concept I had for this book – writing it so I can challenge people like him to try to find out every single day if God is real before they go around saying people who believe in God are unlearned or psychotic. He said he'd take me up on that challenge and actually pray to God for the first time in years.

I added in some more of my testimonies. He was so fascinated that, when my workout on the stair climber ended and we had said our "nice to meet you" to each other, he came to the cross-country ski machine where I was and started talking more – this time revealing that as a teen, he went to church with some neighbors and formed a short-lived relationship with God but he quit believing when several major things didn't happen the way he'd prayed for them to happen.

I told him that, as a teen, I began to doubt for the same reasons too, but that I never allowed that doubt to turn into atheism (well, maybe for about a month, then I became more agnostic). I'm glad I didn't linger in either state of confusion and delusion for too long.

As an adult, I have seen, lost, acquired, read, heard, believed and experienced so much. I really feel bad for people who do not believe in God or do not have the luxury of enjoying the peace of mind only available when you loose your mortal attempts to gain control over a divine situation. I told him that had it not been for Jah, I would probably be dead.

I was quick to show him that I'm not saying God blesses me because I'm trying to look good despite being some hypocritical, pious zealot claiming to have new hands but still condoning select sinful feats. I told him my truth, my personal life's core beliefs regarding spirituality and religion.

I confessed that there are some things I still believe to this day in response to reading the Bible and other literature that I know contradicts what most religions and spiritual organizations teach. I like this because I know that what is good for most is not necessarily good or safe for me in the long run. The biggest thing is that I believe Jah (YHWH, Yahweh) is God and Jesus (Yeshua) is His Son – not God, but is the fulfillment of the promise by God to manifest an aspect of Himself to serve as the Messiah for mankind per the Chosen People's (Black African Hebrew Israelites) request.

The man at the gym said he wasn't sure he could accept that particular belief of mine, but before this conversation with me, he never could understand "the whole 3-n-1 thing" enough to even formulate his own theories.

I told him that my desire to hang on to truth over groups or anything else was another display of innate independence and a love for facts; And because I embraced the thought that I could ask God anything, I didn't listen to a single person who would say to me I "shouldn't question God" – though Jesus said to ASK.

Chapter Three

Experimentation

Accepting that I can't say Jah exists here without working further to prove my claim, I will present several other personal experiences to serve as observations used when I experimented with my hypothesis shortly after forming it years ago. These experimental experiences should also support my hypothesis that God will reveal in time what one wants to, needs to, and prays to know or undergo.

Understanding that, to scientists, this step is normally the one that truly separates science from other disciplines, I will work to be very detailed without being too long winded as I share stories that may prove my hypothesis to you. Each of these situations was treated the exact same way, thus enabling the credibility of the experimental factor of each experience. They each also netted the same result, pretty much.

My first major experiment was conducted when I was about 19 years old. That's when I called on God to keep my friend's car from going over a ledge or ravine with us in it. Loss of control of the vehicle wasn't her fault, and neither of us wanted to die. Thankfully, God answered that prayer IMMEDIATELY.

A couple of weeks before this near-death experience, this good friend (Robrelle McKinley Murray) came to visit me after she had a dream that frightened her. When she arrived, I was hanging out with another of our good friends (Kimera Shanay Funchess, Peace Be Unto this late quintessential, young Southern Queen). Robrelle said the dream she had was that I was in a car with another friend of mine and we were in a terrible car accident that killed us. I told her that would not happen and that the dream may have meant something else.

It was raining heavily the day of the incident, so Robrelle and I were traveling about 20-30 miles per hour because visibility was low on Interstate 55, plus traffic was getting heavy and the road had a lot of water on it. She was ticking along in the left lane when, just after we went under the bridge and was passing the hospital on the hill to our right, her car jerked to the left and we started doing donuts in the grassy median. I know we must have spun around at least three times right off the bat as I prayed, "God please just take care of us," – and, silent in the car, we kept spinning even as I sent up this short prayer. Then, we finally jetted back across the freeway toward the steep ditch at the base of the hospital's hill.

The moment the car reached the shoulder of the road, it came to an abrupt stop. There was no sliding, no hydroplaning, no skidding, nothing – although the street was soaked and traffic was speedy and heavy. I was so thankful.

That's when I asked Robrelle if she was okay. She didn't answer. I asked her a second time. That's when I got a response. She murmured that she was okay. I asked her if she was scratched or anything, and she said she was "thankfully not hurt at all. God is good."

I then got out of the car and walked around it, looking at the tires and checking the body to see if we hit anything in the process of all that. That's when I saw rush hour had already started and the vehicles were coming as though the road was dry. Three other vehicles had pulled over during some point when we were having our experience, and the man in the truck closest to us was running toward our car. I told him we were both fine and the car did not sustain any damage. He returned to his truck as the other drivers waved farewell to us, got back into their rides, and pulled away from the scene.

As Robrelle and I proceeded with our drive without any problems, naturally the talk for the whole ride was about what we'd just gone through together. I reminded her of the dream she'd shared with Shanay and me more than a week prior. I said to Robrelle that I believe the dream was to prepare us both to go through that and rely on God to protect us through it. I told her that the situation probably happened because God allowed it for use to strengthen my faith so I may ask and receive directly, and know that He does love and protect me.

During that experience, I was never afraid for some reason, and I was very calm as I prayed silently. I'm sure Robrelle was calm as she prayed too. Everything happened so quickly that it couldn't have lasted more than a minute or two. I know that it wasn't until the car stopped that I felt the urge to speak or move – but the whole time I knew that no matter what, we would be okay.

I believe this type incident can happen to anybody, and the solution for me and my friend can prove a solution for anybody else. I do not believe that if someone who wanted to live prayed to live that they would die if it is not their time. I used to become upset when I would pray for someone and they died anyway. As an adult, I have learned that my desire for someone's life (and my own) may not be God's purpose or will – and that I cannot stir Jesus to do anything for somebody that a person doesn't want done for himself or herself.

Another experience I'd like to share involves my late friend Shanay in more detail. As you recall, Shanay was the friend present when Robrelle warned me about the dream she had. Maybe it was about a year after Robrelle and I had our experience together that this lesson concerning Shanay took place. Either way, the year was 1996. The month was December and I was 23.

In heavy rain on a Sunday night, while I was at work until close at a pizza delivery spot, Shanay came by to visit me and introduce me to her sister as they waited for their order to finish cooking. I thought they'd lucked up due to their timing, because the phones were quiet the entire time the reunited sisters and I had to spend together before their food was handed to them. But when the phones begin to ring as if the customers saw the long Dominator box go across the counter, I knew our time together was not luck but an appointment (divine, a blessing).

That morning as I slept, I had a dream that two sisters were in an accident with an 18-wheeler on a rainy night and were killed at the intersection of Northside Drive and Medgar Evers. I was awakened from the dream to a call from Robrelle. Her husband, Wesley, who was a new police officer working a fatal car accident he thought involved two teen sisters who are cousins of Shanay's. I told Robrelle to let me call her back because I was having a dream about two sisters who died in a car accident and it might be the same thing.

Time I fell back to sleep deep enough to possibly dream again, my older sister (Latonia) called me and told me to wake up because she had something important to tell me. She said she had her friend (Cookie) on the phone. Cookie is a cousin of Shanay's. She said Shanay and her sister, whom I'd met only seven hours prior, had died in a car accident that a cousin of theirs survived.

I asked them if the accident was with their SUV and an 18-wheeler. They said yes. I then asked if it was in Jackson at Northside and Medgar Evers. They said that yes the accident happened in Jackson, but that it was at West and State streets by the Medgar Evers Post Office in Downtown Jackson. I dropped the phone and began sobbing terribly as so many emotions flooded my body at once. My mother (Susie) and both my younger sisters (Latisha and Richette) came in to console me as I lay curled in the bed lamenting and screaming "no" like crazy.

I believe that Shanay knew that while she was on life support, her sister had died instantly after being beheaded by the collision with the semi-truck's trailer. I believe she knew and that her own lips and nose had been cut off and her shoulders were broken. I believe one of her dying requests was for me to know all this too.

I asked God to strengthen me to be able to deal best with this for the rest of my life, and to enable me to go to see Shanay and her sister during visitation hours at the north Jackson funeral home.

I thanked Jesus for loving my friends and me so much to where power would be used to fulfill a friend's death-bed request to let me know what she and her sister endured in their final moments. And the fact that I was allowed to be told by the narrator of my dream such sensitive details including types of injuries received made me feel like I had been given all the confirmation ever needed to continue to believe God exists and to keep nurturing that divine relationship.

As I sat on the front row after walking past and viewing Shanay and her sister lying in state, being in the funeral chapel alone wasn't creepy to me like I would have guessed it would be. Maybe I was too engulfed in the fact that I am really looking at my friend for the last time, or maybe I was too distraught to have been doing anything in a truly lucid mind anyway; but I surely was getting in what was, to me, my last bit of time with one of my dearest friends. Shanay was also one of the most naturally maternal, feminine, loving and fun-filled souls I have ever been blessed to be influenced by and influence.

When I was leaving, I saw the funeral director and complimented him on his work. I told him that it looked like my friend did her own make-up, and that the eyebrows and logic are the only proofs Shanay didn't dress and make herself up. He accepted the compliment and went on to add that they spent most of their time recreating parts of my friend's face. All I could say was, "I know, and you did a good job," before leaving the funeral home gasping for air and drowning in tears once more.

It took me years to come to terms with Shanay's horrific demise enough to where I could talk about it with someone without slinging snot and salt water, and show them the intense blessing that still came out of it. I also let people know that I celebrate God's answering of my prayer for strength – as it has helped me deal with a number of deaths since Shanay's a lot better than I would have otherwise.

I believe that experience helped me maintain my sensibility and elements of hope, joy and peace when my uncle Alonzo Jefferson (Peace Be Unto this Pharaoh of Kindness and Laughter) was murdered in cold blood back in July 2006. Uncle Lon was a good man. And even today as I weep in writing this due to still dealing with this beloved paternal uncle's undeserved parting and suffering, I do not trick myself into believing that I am sad because his earthly life ended. I know that I am sad because I my preference is still to have him here (despite how jacked up this world and its people are).

Chapter Four

Evaluation

Although both these experiences presented in the last chapter dealt with dreams and car accidents on rainy days, they each had very different outcomes and each show the presence, range and power of God. These life experiments also reveal that no matter who we are or at what point we are in life, sincere prayers backed by faith are answered by God and in accordance to divine will and mortal understanding and choice.

What my observations and experiments revealed about my hypothesis is that while prayers are answered, no one always has prayers answered in the way that they desire – none of us get what we want, when and how we want it, every single time. There have been some prayers of mine that were flat-out not answered and some that have yet to be answered. And because some of the things most desired or felt needed were not delivered to me post prayers, faith and pre-fulfillment testimonies, some people completely will use this lack as a basis to entirely dismiss my hypothesis that God will prove He exists if someone sincerely prays and really wants to know the facts of a faith or anything else. But then, all people routinely doubt self, others and God, so this is nothing new or some reaction unique to my disclosure.

My requirement to grasp the factual in order to fully embrace the sacred, faithful or religious is a commonality many believers and non-believers share. This is why so many people cite contradictions in the Bible as their reason for disbelief, while others rattle off unanswered prayers and disappointing times in life as their reasons to reject God's existence. It shows that whether positive or negative, exposure does not guarantee proper attention, but mainly provides an opportunity for notice.

Life has few guarantees and little to be offered as an absolute with an universal application. But, no matter how bad any point in any life is, everybody else has felt that way too because of something not working out the way they wanted it.

Every body suffers some hurt or loss from time to time that is felt to have shattered reality and changed livelihood. Some of us are able to learn from it and move on in a positive way, while there are some of us who move on in a negative way.

I contend that, no matter how much anything hurts or makes us angry, we should not lie and deny God exists. Imagine having your identity deleted from government files and no longer receiving a paycheck all because you did not do some illegal things that people wanted you to do.

Anything against God's will is more than likely illegal and/or sinful, so no one is right to harbor ill feelings about God behind any thing left undone that was expected or desired to be done. What is right is to be thankful despite situations – even if for no other reason than the fact that things can always be worse.

Neither science, metaphysics, inability nor bad times can excuse any of us from praising Jah – and none definitely qualify any of us to be correct in denying God lives. After all, just because somebody doesn't like the content of this book does not mean this tome does not exist and I did not sit here and type in every word as it occurred to my brain.

In the last chapter, I talked about one of my horrific and meaningful near-death experiences and the way holy intervention changed the outcome in a number of ways for Robrelle and me. Additionally, I discussed a separate experience where my very close friend Shanay and her sister were killed, and the miraculous way I learned the details of their fatal traffic accident. Both these experiences strengthened my belief in God and in my god-self aspect. By accepting myself as a Goddess, I am not insinuating I am omnipotent or omniscient, but I am pointing out the awareness and acceptance of the God in me and my thankfulness for the increased capability that brings.

No matter how someone might try to explain the meanings of these incidents as something other than what they were, these experiences and their truths remain unchanged. Sight does not override existence, regardless how heavily it serves as the determinant of reality for many.

Each time my hypothesis that God will reveal Himself when pursued is tested against the available data, it doesn't matter the angle taken or any tangents followed, the belief that God will prove He exists to those who ask always holds water more often than it spills milk.

Praying to know a thing, be protected, gain a skill, or have a thing confirmed has always proven to be a beneficial tactic for my life. Praying to know God is real and I can call on Her and be directed by Him will always be the things that led to my reading the mounds of books and closely watching the thousands of people that I did that proved to me God exists (although a number of them were presented in ways meant to prove there was no such entity).

Considering this, I must state for the record that even if I never get another prayer answered, I am faithful that my conviction that what was proven has been well proven and will probably enable me to still believe in Jehovah and Jesus no matter what (because that's what faith is – belief without proof that your belief is a fact).

The path of proving God exists in one form or another is not an experience reserved for the elite religion traditionalists. Being a young adult without regular church attendance who is as sinful as the most righteous people and less sinful than the most wicked, I believe God does not play favors – no matter how some churchgoers claim He does. God's preference will only come into play during the Tribulation and on Judgment Day. Things prior are more human choice with a lot of consequences and rewards mixed in with a large helping of God's forgiveness, blessings, lessons, and protection.

This chapter's evaluation of personal experiences / experiments have displayed what my observation of these encounters revealed to me and how they were interpreted by me – with no facts skewed and no details exaggerated. But, before I declare it a scientific fact and label it as a theory, I'd like to observe a few other experiences of varying weight than these already presented, then compare and contrast that data and present my evaluation in this upcoming chapter.

In doing so, I will actively attempt to bring additional balance and observation that some readers may want and expect. This will also serve to display that my hypothesis is not a statement solely based on my near-death experiences but also the experiences with less automatic intensity that prove God answers all kinds of prayers throughout a person's life. Therefore, it is only natural that I now present to you other first-hand knowledge that shows my belief in God is not as much built around life-saving situations as it is a faith built upon life-affirming situations.

Chapter Five

Testing

With these tertiary observations of experimental experiences, I seek to show you more scenes from the movie that's my life as I test, for myself and you, whether the information gained during this and previous series of tests is mostly contrary to data previously collected, or if my hypothesis is solid and I can move forward confidently and accept my hypothesis as a fact.

Let me again say: I know how painful it can be when desires and requirements go unfulfilled. Everybody knows how it feels to be in physical and emotional pain – even a child knows. I remember that it was when I was a child that I first experienced an awareness of the difference between answered and unanswered prayers. But, it wasn't until I became an adult that I understood possible reasons why prayers are/not answered.

God has done so much more for me than I can name. And while there are some things that you and I both know I desire that I have yet to acquire, the things I can rattle off the top of my head that represent unfulfilled prayers are miniscule compared to the miracles and blessings I've received. It's like three pages compared to 3,000. Check yours out. We're probably not very different – more a blessed creation than an abandoned angelic animal.

Last year, I was on the tail end of my six-hour drive to Mississippi when my SUV broke down in Louisiana despite my praying to make it to my mom's without problems. The incident I had ANYWAY delayed my arrival by three hours, but at least I made it there safely and highway patrol and a local gravel hauler kept watch on me as they traveled east and west on 20 while I was there. They even blew as they passed when Jamison Towing (sent by my sister Tonia) was loading my Isuzu Rodeo to take me and it on to Jackson. I guess that makes my prayer to make it to my mom's answered after all, so 50% fulfillment on a prayer isn't bad at all in my book. But just in case it doesn't spread the mustard for you, I'll come up with another, more solid unanswered prayer example and resume writing in a moment.

Okay. An unanswered prayer of mine is my prayer to become a multi-millionaire who has helped at least 10 other people become a millionaire by the time I turn 30. Well, I turned 34 in May and am no multi-millionaire. And, although I have helped make companies multi-millions and individuals hundreds of thousands,

I am no multi-millionaire. I am saving to buy my first home and make my less than 45k busting my butt working through my own companies and servicing individuals and companies with some of everything including journalism, accounting assistance, marketing SOQs, custom design and printing, and first-tier technical end-user support.

Please, don't get me wrong. I am not overall bitter about this outcome. My prayers for and faith in that financial experience were not honored in the time frame I wanted it fulfilled in, but I still have faith that I will become wealthy one day and my mother will never have to work another day in her life in order to pay bills and survive with a lot fewer worries about herself, her family, her friends, and strangers in need. Right now, I am remaining faithful that my financial situation will change and I am thankful for the fact that I don't have to be treated any dog kind of way just to TRY to make sure I get a paycheck when the next cycle rolls around.

Now, while I might not be able to come up with flat out negative examples of unanswered prayers, I can come up with flat out positive examples of answered prayers. My mother, for example, has almost died a dozen times that I know of, and probably more times that I don't know about. I will only mention a few of them here (for the sake of book price due to page count) to testify that prayers and faith have been honored for the most part in my life and the lives of those who love me and whom I love.

The first time Momma almost died, she was 35 and had two aneurysms in her head. The small one vanished years later, but the big one had ballooned and was leaking that first moment we witnessed her almost die. For the past four years, she hasn't given us a scare – but the last time she did it was from complications of myastenia gravis.

This year my Earth Mother turned 58, but she looks like a 38-year-old whose hair turned gray early. And while some people can look at her and tell she is sickly and has gained weight due to medications, she gets around like a lady who hasn't been sick a single day in her life, let alone sick enough to stop breathing as you're looking at her. That's just a little bit about this Supreme Goddess and the power of God in her life. The entire story is so profound that it will be its own book (visit www.bepublished.biz periodically to check for that book's release this year – if she follows the schedule like I keep pressing her to because so many more people can be helped by her testimonies and inspired by her life).

See, not only did God answer those prayers from my mother and her family to take care of her, His Holy Spirit even moved on my behalf when I suddenly needed a scholarship just to make sure I start school when I wanted.

After being recruited by schools including the Massachusetts Institute of Technology, I applied to and was accepted by Spellman College. With no money saved for college and not enough coming in grants, I asked God to help me get a scholarship from Jackson State University so I could start school there two days after I graduate high school.

My mother told me God showed her to send me to talk to Charles Boler (Peace Be Unto this late youth and education advocate who was my father by virtue of eternal and unconditional support, development and love for me from ages 14-34). Papa Chuck was the director of Upward Bound at JSU. He called Trent Walker and asked Trent to expect me in his office so he can take me to Dr. Maria Harvey who was over the JSU's Honor's College. I didn't know Trent before that day and he didn't know me, but he complied with Mr. Boler and took me to see Dr. Harvey. Another conduit of Our Maker, Dr. Harvey talked to me, reviewed my transcript, and scraped together me a partial scholarship from funds left over after they'd awarded all the full and partials for the upcoming fall semester. With that extra needed bit obtained, I was able to start JSU that summer, and two days after graduating Jim Hill High School because the Upward Bound Bridge Program paid for me to take two classes during that session.

Another time, I prayed that if I am to take a certain dream I had as a divine message literally or figuratively expressed that I would see a certain sequence of events happen that were totally out of my control – and they happened. Here's my rundown of what I asked for and what came to pass: (1) Maxwell comes out with another R&B CD; (2) he schedules a tour but does not initially include Dallas; (3) he adds a Dallas show to his tour and a friend of mine gets free tickets; (4) my friend immediately calls me and invites me to go to the show with her; and (5) Maxwell takes notice of me and it cannot be denied.

All those things happened a year or so after the prayer was sent up and the expectation of fulfillment began. When my friend (Shani Scott, author of The Rough Side/The Soft Side) called me one Tuesday and asked me what I was doing that Saturday, I told her that I was going with her to the Maxwell concert at the Bronco Bowl in Dallas. That's when I added in details about the prayer. She then told me that after Maxwell put out his "Now" CD, he arranged a tour but didn't have Dallas on it at first – and that when he added Dallas the show instantly sold out, so he added on a second show (which was a little different from my request, but still) and we had tickets to that second show!

At the concert, Shani nearly elbowed my right arm to death as she was saying, "He's looking right at you. He's singing to you, Girl!" I didn't believe her, so I made that childhood mean mug and licked out my tongue as I put my hands on my hips and rolled my neck as a test to see if he was really looking at me. He must have been because he suddenly smiled harder and ran to the other side of the stage, sat down, and continued singing while looking at me. Naysayers may claim he was only looking in my direction and he was not looking at me – which is the same thing I originally thought. They are extremely incorrect, just as I was completely in disbelief.

Within days of the concert, I'd received several calls from people saying that Maxwell's girlfriend was at the concert and he kept looking at her during this one particular song. I allowed the conversation to go the same way with each of them before I interjected my question at almost the same point in each person's soliloquy. And when they described what the lady looked like, I told them that was me and not some woman from New York who's already his girlfriend.

To prove it to them, I told them all where I was positioned. I then reminded them that what I wore that night to the concert was nothing new but was something I put together from stuff I'd been wearing for years around them. I threw in a few more facts for them, like the name of the friend I was with at the concert. Shani happens to be someone all of them know. Quickly for some and eventually for others, they each knew that I was the one standing in an afro wig with white jeans, black boots and a red leather coat as Maxwell serenaded me before thousands. But more than that for me, they each confirmed that my prayer for this was answered well beyond its entirety.

Chapter Six

Theory

It is my belief that the several of many observations and experiences shared here has allowed you to see that there is no limit to God's power.

If not for consideration for pricing of this book, I probably would have been on Page 850 before it was time to almost bring this ministry tool to a close.

If nothing else, what I most want to convey is my thought that anyone who wants to know what they need to know – about God, Jah, Jesus, Yeshua, The Holy Spirit, Moses, Adam, Math, Science, Underwater Basket Weaving or anything else – can just ask to know or experience, or understand, or tolerate, or get over (again, sincerely ask whatever).

He or she should also be faithful about receipt while also being willing to work to attain the desired and implement its truths into daily life. We're all better off anyway any time we are living a life utilizing knowledge gained from past experiences to assure improved encounters and diminish general complications in life.

When any of us take the time to look at our lives, our overall experience will not differ much. Recalling and accepting the lessons throughout my life was not an easy journey.

At one point during the time of adolescence when I was going through my agnostic phase, I prayed to not have dreams because I wasn't sure which dreams would come true and which were just dreams. They stopped until I prayed for them to return almost a year later when I felt I could handle them better. Yes, by then the agnostic phase (which lasted a few years by the way) was ending, but I mentioned that as an example of something that I have gone through that most people have not, but that most people can still relate to on some level due to something they have experienced or observed.

And just like people have these type things and many other things in common, people also share a common ability to know God and help others realize God exists. Any of us can tell as many people as we want to that faithful prayer is the science that proves God is real, and to feel free to experiment with Jesus.

I believe that the Holy Spirit helped me see that God/Jah is the real source of all life and has manifested as our Messiah and is therefore called Jesus/Yeshua by Christians/Hebrew Israelites.

My theory is that anyone doubting God exists can sincerely pray to know the truth about this question and anything else desired or required.

It doesn't matter if a person is in Japan, Jalisco or Jasper – all prayers have the possibility to be answered to the satisfaction of the person praying, working and believing.

It doesn't matter if a person is Chilean, cheating, homicidal, or a homosexual – their sincere and fervent prayers have just as much a chance of being heard and answered as any priest's or pope's.

I was taught that the only person having that unique access to The Almighty is The Son. Nevertheless, each of us do have a direct portal to God everywhere we go.

We must keep our relationship with God alive. Life is far better with God than without

God – because you and I both know that if it was not for my belief in God, I would not be happy or optimistic about life overall since there are still some dire wants yet to be fulfilled.

Chapter Seven

Conclusion

Observing and assessing life experiences, I concluded that when people say Yahweh is the real source of all life that the statement is accurate.

If God is real, then God is all powerful. If God is all powerful, then God can create human beings (a fact I find a lot more believable than monkeys turning into people, especially since there are no newly-turned humans being found in jungles around the world).

And while I have no personal affinity for the scientific method, I chose it as a guide of sorts for use to organize my experiences into evidence that can test and support God's existence. I pray this work does not incite scientists to riot because of my loose application of these methods of the scientific approach.

I understand that, to scientists, the scientific method as a whole is the best way to decipher fact from fiction.

I only wonder why they haven't used it for the same purposes regarding God (be sure to let me know if I am incorrect in that assumption).

In trying to make my point that Creator God of the Original People still lives, I followed these five steps from scientific methods: observation, hypothesis, experimentation, evaluation, testing, and theory.

I accept that some may argue that my hypothesis and resulting theory have no official validity because my testing and experimentation were based on spiritual experiences that are only able to be substantiated but not proven.

Others may dismiss this book as something that shows nothing more than people see what we want to see.

Any person subscribing to such thoughts deprives only himself or herself of their fullest potential, because it is only through God that they can do things they normally are unable to do (and know things they otherwise would not know).

New ideas have always had a hard time getting acceptance from individuals and the masses.

The burden of proof that God exists lies not on any person or on any entity, rather on a single act – FAITH.

Also, there is present a process that allows everybody to have practical proof, and that is PRAYER.

But, all in all, I believe that even a brief a look at your life and mine will reveal to the world enough SCIENTIFIC EVIDENCE GOD EXISTS.

Artist's Profile

Ronny Myles, a Texan residing in Atlanta, illustrated the cover art – which is actually a portion of his piece, "September 11, 2001." The husband and father creates beautiful, expressive works covering multiple themes with various mediums, and also accepts commissions. *artbyronE.com*

Author's Biography

The third of five children, Mylia Tiye Mal Jaza is a native of Mississippi who has lived in Texas since first moving from Jackson to Arlington in 1997.

A professional writer for most of her life, Mylia first began charging fellow elementary school students who requested she write songs, poems, letters and essays for them. Although never published, she wrote her first book (All About Cindy) at the age of eight. By high school graduation, she was already writing college research papers and providing thesis assistance to graduate students.

During her second year at Jackson State University, Mylia had begun working in print media as a copy editor for *The West Jackson Journal*. It was near the end of that spring semester that she began working as an obituary writer with Mississippi's largest newspaper, *The Clarion-Ledger*. By the close of that following fall semester, she was a staff reporter covering various beats. She also briefly freelanced as a news reporter for the *Jackson Advocate* (Peace Be Unto the late pioneer and brave heart Charles Tisdale who died July 2007).

Mylia completed undergraduate studies at JSU in 1996, receiving a Bachelor's of Science degree in Mass Communications. With her concentration as Broadcast Journalism and her minor as English, she graduated a few classes shy of receiving a second bachelor's degree in English with a minor in Speech. However, before relocating to Texas in 1997, Mylia was not only a solid journalist but had also accumulated impressive public speaking, vocal performance, and broadcasting experience by introducing various Who's Who during special ceremonies around Jackson, singing during talent shows and weddings, working briefly at JSU's vintage and smooth jazz radio station (WJSU), and interning in 1996 at the state's top television station (WLBT-3).

After arriving in Dallas/Fort Worth, Mylia formed her own "communications firm" and was soon hired by the *Arlington Morning News* and *Dallas Morning News* as a staff writer, and by *The Dallas Examiner* as a managing editor. There, she established an internship program that awarded college credit, and helped the weekly win more awards than it reportedly had ever won during a single year. Mylia has also written for magazines and newspapers including *Eclipse Magazine, Teen Graffiti* and *Intercessors for Christ.*

In 1998, she moved from Arlington to Dallas after taking on a finance/accounting recruiting position with an international staffing agency. For the company, she also produced a monthly newsletter and recruited and staffed for its healthcare division, as well as provided advertising design/copywriting and creation and implementation of trade shows/participation, special in-house events, and nurse certification programs.

Post recruiting for another staffing firm specializing in Human Resources, Mylia was introduced to the architectural / engineering / construction / environmental / water resources fields when she began extending corporate communications, marketing, recruiting, technical writing, and presentation compilation services to small businesses and medium corporations in 2001.

In May 2002, she enrolled at the University of Texas at Dallas to obtain a Master's degree. In December 2003, she was one of two students to be awarded a Master of Arts & Humanities from UTD. So doing, she possibly became the first African-American student to be awarded a professional / terminal MAH from the college's program.

Since forming The Writers Consortium and The Sitting Room in 1997, Mylia has completed a number of tasks through all eight of her companies.

With **The Sitting Room**, she completes tasks ranging from devising and implementing market research questionnaires and response analysis to data entry and website construction.

ARTiculation is the company through which she provides broadcasting services inclusive of writing and performing voice-overs for phone systems and web casts.

She has also established herself within the Metroplex community as a local artist by showing her abstract and still art work, and performing music and poetry, after booking shows in Dallas-area venues through her company **PeopleWarmers**.

Additionally, she helps others with creative expression services via **The Writers Consortium**; support services such as image consulting, apparel design, and diction coaching via **Jefferson-Taylor**; community outreach, mentoring, tutoring, and charitable donations via **Life's Purpose Ministries**; with self-publishing assistance and self-promotions training via **BePublished**; and various business communications, human resources, accounting and marketing services via **The Conglomerate**.

One with a vision of opening a tea room and small chain of all-suite themed hotels, Mylia is the author and/or editor of seven of her own published works to date:

<u>Life Is Beautiful: La Vita E Bella</u>

<u>Life Is Beautiful: La Vita Es Hermosa</u>

<u>Seen In Other Words</u>

<u>Plea For Peace</u>

<u>The Old Negro and The New Negro by T. LeRoy Jefferson, M.D.</u>

<u>All for Show: Film & Television Scripts</u>

<u>Scientific Evidence God Exists</u>

Under the name Goddess Sage, she has also recorded music with a number of other artists, had her performance included on underground and promotional mixed CDs, and has her own CD available (a six-song EP titled "Freedom Found"). Mylia is also known by select original art aficionados as the visual abstract and still art expressionist Sun Child Wind Spirit.

Order Form

Thank you for your support.

Life Is Beautiful:
La Vita E Bella
$16.95 x _____

The Old Negro and
The New Negro by
T. LeRoy Jefferson M.D.
_____ x $20/hard
_____ x $10/soft

Life Is Beautiful:
La Vita Es Hermosa
$12.95 x _____

All For Show:
Film & Television Scripts
_____ x $25

Seen In Other Words
$8.95 x _____

Plea For Peace
_____ x $8.95

"Freedom Found" EP/CD
Goddess Sage
$10.50 x _____

Scientific Evidence
God Exists
_____ x $30/hard
_____ x $20/soft

ORDER TOTAL + $5 shipping/handling $ _____ . _____

READER _____

ADDRESS _____ UNIT # _____

CITY _____ ST _____ ZIP _____

EMAIL _____ COUNTY _____ COUNTRY _____

Please Remit Payment & Form To
Mylia Jaza
P.O. Box 8324
Jackson, MS 39284-8324

Please allow four (4) weeks for order delivery to allow processing and autographing.

Order Form

Thank you for your support.

Life Is Beautiful:
La Vita E Bella
$16.95 x _____

The Old Negro and
The New Negro by
T. LeRoy Jefferson M.D.
_____ x $20/hard
_____ x $10/soft

Life Is Beautiful:
La Vita Es Hermosa
$12.95 x _____

All For Show:
Film & Television Scripts
_____ x $25

Seen In Other Words
$8.95 x _____

Plea For Peace
_____ x $8.95

"Freedom Found" EP/CD
Goddess Sage
$10.50 x _____

Scientific Evidence
God Exists
_____ x $30/hard
_____ x $20/soft

ORDER TOTAL + $5 shipping/handling $ _____ . _____

READER _____

ADDRESS _____ UNIT # _____

CITY _____ ST _____ ZIP _____

EMAIL _____ COUNTY _____ COUNTRY _____

Please Remit Payment & Form To
Mylia Jaza
P.O. Box 8324
Jackson, MS 39284-8324

Please allow four (4) weeks for order delivery to allow processing and autographing.

Order Form

Thank you for your support.

Life Is Beautiful:
La Vita E Bella
$16.95 x _____

The Old Negro and
The New Negro by
T. LeRoy Jefferson M.D.
_____ x $20/hard
_____ x $10/soft

Life Is Beautiful:
La Vita Es Hermosa
$12.95 x _____

All For Show:
Film & Television Scripts
_____ x $25

Seen In Other Words
$8.95 x _____

Plea For Peace
_____ x $8.95

"Freedom Found" EP/CD
Goddess Sage
$10.50 x _____

Scientific Evidence
God Exists
_____ x $30/hard
_____ x $20/soft

ORDER TOTAL + $5 shipping/handling $ _____ . _____

READER _____

ADDRESS _____ UNIT # _____

CITY _____ ST _____ ZIP _____

EMAIL _____ COUNTY _____ COUNTRY _____

Please Remit Payment & Form To
Mylia Jaza
P.O. Box 8324
Jackson, MS 39284-8324

Please allow four (4) weeks for order delivery to allow processing and autographing.

Softcover ISBN: 978-0-6151-6333-8

www.ingramcontent.com/pod-product-compliance
Lightning Source LLC
LaVergne TN
LVHW011407080426
835511LV00005B/428